# A SIMPLISTIC LEADERSHIP APPROACH

Practical Leadership Systems for all levels

SEAN M. SUGGS

*It starts with having an open mind to change or
your mind will be changed for you*

*Sean Marcellas*

OK, I know the cover is a little overwhelming but hang in there
and I promise it gets better!

If you give me 1 or 2 hours, I will give you all you need to know
about how to become a great leader regardless of what business,
job, career, or leadership position you may currently hold or
someday aspire to have.

It will start with forgetting all of those 500-page leadership books
that have been read, and the endorsed management classes taken
about how to become an effective leader while paying thousands
of dollars trying to find the magic. Some of them are very good but
I would like to suggest taking this book out while on a lunch break
and begin implementing change today. With 50 pages only, it can
be done!

What makes me an expert on leadership? It is derived from my belief, experience and background. I am a Christian and a father of 6 children (5 girls and 1 boy) between the ages of 21 and 30 years old. I have had 8 years of military experience with achieving the rank of Army Sergeant. I've worked as a sales and marketing representative in the gaming industry, worked for one of the top pharmaceutical company in the US, held a position as Residence Hall Director at a university responsible for 350 freshmen, and I have 19 years of automotive experience starting from a line team leader to a Senior Executive. During my career I have led teams of 5 to 2,500+. I have served on at least 20 boards of directors across America and I received my MBA from Auburn University. (War Eagle!) Finally, behind every great leader is a wonderful partner, and I have been very fortunate to have the support of my wife. Has this sparked your interest? Want to learn more?

My first request will be the most important request of the entire book. If you don't wake up every morning with a *smile* on your face and a firm belief that your team will make a significant difference today due to your leadership, you should stop reading this book and perhaps change jobs. Leadership is not for the meek. It's a role that is life changing and should inspire others to achieve their personal goals. Managers will not understand this. Managers count value and Leaders create value & Leaders Lead people versus Managers managing work! HBR

Leadership requires taking the narrow path and liking it. It requires being the least recognized member of the team and liking it. Humility is an essential part of leadership. It requires you to have a Twitter mindset and not a Pterodactyl mindset. In other words, you must be progressive and not rely on practices you used for the past 20 or 30 years because we all know what happened to the Pterodactyl.

So let's get started!

Clearly, the title of this book generated enough interest for you to read this far and determine if it can take you places that will allow you to excel as a leader and feel good about making a difference. Whether you are a freshman leader just learning how to lead or the most senior leader trying to rid yourself of the old mindset and ready to open your mind to new innovative ideas.

This learning session will cover 9 core components that will guide you on your daily journey becoming a world class leader. I have also included some very practical examples that you can start using today.

> *A leader is best when people barely know he exists,*
> *when his work is done, his aim fulfilled, they will*
> *say: we did it ourselves.*
>
> *— Lao Tzu*

*Morale is your Company's Manifest Destiny*

*Sean Marcellas*

Chapters:

| | | |
|---|---|---|
| **K** | - | Kindle (Spark–Ignite-Touch) |
| **I** | - | Intellect (Understanding - Capable- Mental Agility) |
| **S** | - | Simply Lead (No seriously, Simply Lead) |
| **S** | - | Servant Lead (Moves more rocks than a bulldozer) |
| **M** | - | Money Maker! (You must get results) |
| **Y** | - | You (If you don't do it, you don't believe it) |
| **@** | - | Attitude (The Engine) |
| **#** | - | Systems (Sustainable, growth, legacy...) |
| **$** | - | Succession (You need to be an Elevator Operator) |

# K – KINDLE

## (Spark-Ignite-touch)

I am of the opinion that a great leader is better seen and not heard. I believe that in order to become or develop as a great leader; you must have the ability to *kindle* the organization, team, or small group. This is a must in your first 30 days of leading a team. If you blow this opportunity, you will be swimming upstream for a long time.

Here are some practical things that you can do.

Remember these five things:

1. In your 1-hour introduction meeting: 75% of your discussion should be about the type of person you are and what motivates you as a leader. 25% should focus on how you will help the team.

2.   You should meet with your team members first, not your boss. ---- Set-up a team building activity during the first week (I know who does that, right? Well you do now!)

3.   Your first calendar entries should be the birthdays and anniversary dates of your direct report team members.

4.   Learn the company's mission and vision in detail. Why does it exist? How have they tried to live it?

5.   Great leaders can assess talent in one week --- you have to do this early to detect who is there for a Job and who is there for a Career?

1. Intros are the launching pad!  It's that first impression thing that everyone talks about. Just remember, the impression you make as a leader has a significant impact.

   a.   Your team is probably thinking some of the following:

       1.   Here we go again!

       2.   Why didn't I get the job as a leader?

       3.   I don't believe his or her resume is accurate.

       4.   Change is coming!

       5.   I am so excited that so and so is gone!

       6.   Another black person!

       7.   Another white person!

       8.   Another woman!

       9.   Finally they got it right!

       10.  Man I have to prove myself all over again.

As you can see, your new team has a wide spectrum of thoughts. Here are few pointers to bring these diverse ideas together

       1.   Be yourself - They can smell a fake a mile away

       2.   Keep it 100% - Always tell the truth. If you don't know it, tell them you don't know it.

       3.   Talk about your life, not your work strategy. Team member respect leaders who talk about family first.

       4.   Ask questions. Play a game where each person must ask one exploratory question about you.

5.   Leave them with your personal philosophy. You must leave them thinking about a positive thought; i.e. "I promise to work my tail off for each of you, and I will listen to your opinion on projects and processes." As opposed to: "We are going to achieve our goals no matter what it takes." Your team will think of you as a task driven crazy person if you start out that way.

*   Always leave them with a smile! No matter what the situation is, leaving on a positive note will build a culture of teamwork and focus.

**2.** Why the team first and not the boss? Well, 99% of the time, your boss hired you and knows all about you so don't waste your time trying to impress him or her; it's your team you need to make a great first impression with. You do this by utilizing the listening rule. The meeting should consist of 75% listening and 25% responding. The first one-on-one session or group session should convey you as the best listener they have ever seen.

Focus on what is important to each team member. In the future, this will be a tremendous benefit to both you and the company while striving to achieve the organization's goals and objectives.

**3.** We all have the urge to place all of the important meetings on our calendars as soon as we get to the work place. We meet the new Administrative Associate and instruct the individual to fill it up! This means your calendar will go from 0 to 60 in 3 seconds. If you want to make a good impression on your staff, set some priorities about what is important to your team. Your first request to your Administrative Associate should be to populate your calendar with all the birthdays and work anniversaries of all of your Direct Reports.

Saying "Happy Birthday" or "Happy Anniversary" to your team members is priceless and will give you immediate street credibility that you care. Just think about how you feel when your boss never says happy birthday to you?

**4.** Learning the company's mission and vision can make your job a lot easier. If it doesn't exist, you need to create a direction for the team. If companies paid closer attention to the mission/vision statement, and tied the organizational objectives to it, employees would be much happier. This correlation should be evaluated throughout each step of the process to determine whether or not it will help the team bring about the mission.

Needless to say, just having a great mission/vision statement is only the first step. The next step, of course is the execution! This is done through rewarding team members who actively demonstrate the values of the company in their day to day dealings with other people. Again, you are trying to *kindle* the company with your team's key actions.

Lastly, you may be the person who has to build the mission/vision. If that is case, it gives you a great opportunity to create true team work by building it together.

## █ SPEAKING OF VISION:

You must have a Mission and Vision --- If you don't --- Stop and flip to the appendix on setting a good mission and vision and make one. (No matter the size of your team)  Your road map has to be clear to get your team to follow. Some of the worst leaders I have ever had did not have a road map. They shot from the hip daily. I called them Pterodactyl' and we know what happened to them, right?

**5.** Spotting the Slash and Splash. Sean-ism A few years ago the Pittsburgh Steelers had a quarterback named Cornell Stewart. His coach nick-named him Slash. Why you may ask? Well, Cornell had a very unique talent of performing several jobs on the team in addition to that of quarterback.  Recognizing the Cornell's in your team is essential to achieving the goals and objectives of your business. They are typically what we may call a "Steady Eddie" or SME-Subject Matter Expert type of a person. If Cornell Stewart is the Slash of the NFL, Tom Brady (4 time Super Bowl Champ) is the Splash.  The Splash person(s) are the two or three team members, and I do mean the two or three team members, who will out work everyone else and see things that the average team member just can't see. Understanding and identifying these members will benefit you significantly as you try to build the weakest link to a strong team member. They are the future of your company and create a solid foundation for its success.

Once you find them, recognize them, pay them for what they are worth and make sure they are in your foxhole on a daily basis. Who are your *Slash* and *Splash* team members? What have you done to make them feel valued today?  Who in the organization, based on your quick assessment, is "Pushing the rope or pulling the rope?"

The first 30 days on the job are very important to set the tone for your company, team or group. I believe Colin Powell's phrase, "After 30 days you own the sheets" This means that if after the first 30 days, you haven't succeeded in setting the tone, you will ultimately be responsible for the outcomes.

If you fail to set the tone, all the talk about your predecessor or what happened in the past will be forgotten, and the emphasis will be solely on what you did (or didn't do).

Did you notice that I never mentioned your boss giving you an orientation schedule or 90-day attack plan or a specific project to complete?  Why? Well, it's simple; if you understand the five facets of "Kindle" and implement them, there is really no need for an orientation.  Most companies do not give you a road map so you may have to create your own. **(See Appendix for example if you need it--- first 90 days)**

Last thing to remember when you are trying to Kindle an organization, "Do not try to accomplish more that you and your team can handle." It's a common mistake that a lot of leaders make in the first year on the job. We try to get 1,000 things done in a short period of time before we have done a thorough job of assessing the team's capability, the company's capabilities and most importantly is the climate or culture ready for all of the these great ideas that you have?  Don't out kick your coverage!

The more you can create **trust**; you can create **thrust** for your team! If your team does not have the belief in you then everything you try will be a challenge.  Kindle starts trust building which is essential for building initial trust.

# I – INTELLECT

## (Understanding - Capable- Mental Agility)

All great leaders bring different skill sets to the table.  Some will out work you; some will have strong technical abilities while others will have a great ability to get things done with great team work skills.

Regardless of which category you fall under, you must have the capacity to learn and comprehend the business. For progressive companies, the days of good ole boys getting promotions and underperforming are over. If you are going to make a significant impact, you can't just "fake it to make it" forever. It will catch up to you long term.

Let's say you are fortunate enough to get a great leadership position, but you are uncertain about how you should lead this group, team or company due to your lack of complete knowledge of the company or job. What do you do?

## KEY POINTS:

1. Remember money is not made in your office or at your desk. Go to the source to find the facts to make correct/important decisions

2. Learn one or two floor level jobs yourself ---- Build some credibility. This allows you get a deep understanding of what truly makes your team members tick on a daily basis.

3. Be a continuous learner – Benchmark --- find the great leaders and mimic what they are doing --- Shamelessly Steal!

4. Have a Mentor –You need one no matter what level you are in your career ---- This will get you off to a flying start and keep the ship running when you get in a pinch.

5. Hone your listening skills and ask questions—from those simple ones like where is the bathroom to the more complex questions of how does your team develop its engineering drawings?

1. Please remember that there is no money made in your office, all the money is made on the production floor, the design floor, or the research floor.  OK, I think you get it. Great leader's practice a concept used in the Toyota world called Genchi Genbutsu. This means no matter what leadership level you hold; you go to

the source to find out the detailed information needed to make important decisions.

Do not be the person who only uses conference rooms to make decisions. Haven't we all seen enough PowerPoints?

This will also give you the ability to verify systems, development opportunities and get the pulse of the company in real-time.

**2.** As I mentioned at the beginning of Kindle, great leaders are seen not heard.  One of your goals should be to learning one or two freshmen jobs in your area of responsibility. That goes for you as well Mr. or Ms. CEO! This will build your credibility in the company. This will build your street cred in the company. You should have a "beginner's mindset about your role. It will go a long way for several different reasons. One of the most important reasons is that now, when faced with making executive decisions, you will be able to understand and appreciate the impact the members in the plant make to the company overall, as well as how your decision may affect them.

**3.** Being a continuous learner starts with realizing that someone else may have a better way of doing things or better ideas within your company or outside your company's walls. Most team members love to be challenged with a new approach or thinking to simplify their jobs.  With the **speed of innovation and trends**, you will get left behind each year if you do not continue to grow. Use technology to get things done. Do not wait for manual knowledge building if a technical system can do it faster and better.

Your advancement will depend on you taking the organization to a new level.

Ideas for the continuous learner:

1. Find a great leader and copy their style.

2. Read, Read, and Read some more--- What's new or upcoming? Remember Twitter or Pterodactyl? You must stay up to date on **innovation and trends**

3. Most importantly, you should always have diversity in mind. The Millennials will not be led the same way as you may have led just last year. Learn from them.

**4.** When I think of a mentor, I think of a person who walks alongside of us, someone that listens to you, a mature person and a person with wisdom. **"A leader is one that goes the way, knows the way and shows the way"** John Maxwell

When I need a word of encouragement or a motivating push, I call one my mentors. I know that they will assess the situation and always shoot me straight. I think a strong leader who I really enjoy reading about is Tony Dungy.  Tony was the first African American coach to win a super bowl.  "When mentor leaders demonstrate their loyalty time and time again to those they lead – in both their personal and professional lives, those relationships will be fortified to withstand whatever challenges they face."Tony Dungy

> "If you are wise, you will use your mentor as a spring board not just a conversation piece" It should be purposeful! Sean-ism

## 5. Listening and Questions

"Great leaders are extremely mindful of their surroundings. They know how to actively listen beyond the obvious via both verbal and non-verbal communication. They acknowledge others through body language, facial expressions and nods. These types of leaders possess a tremendous degree of executive presence and are tuned in to the dynamics that are taking place around them, at all times." (HBR)

You must be intentional with your listening skills to gather the information that will help you make decisions. You can't be everywhere all the time so you must be strategic to know when to listen to the right people at the right time. This is skill that is developed over time and will produce dividends long term.

Questions are also very important but should only be asked once strong listening has occurred. This means if you can be patient during an entire conversation your questions may be answered. It's been said over and over again, the leader is not the smartest person in the organization. If you are not the smartest, you must listen to the smartest and ask probing questions that will continue to have those members share their insight to propel the organization. When difficult decisions have to be made, you should pull in the key players to support making the right decision.

As the leader, everyone is watching your every move and action. If you appear disconnected, you are perceived as disinterested and not listening. Never stop being expansively mindful.

"Keep an open mind and press rewind" Sean-ism

You should listen and be able to recite the key points back to the person. This will build relationship deposits and will give your team members confidence that you will listen and take action.

# S - SIMPLY LEAD

## keep it simple, It's OK

Okay, enough of 5 key topics; we are going to keep it simple with only 3!!!

The best leaders that I have ever been fortunate enough to encounter had the following 3 critical traits to keep it simple.

## MODELING

Great leaders lead by example every day, remember there is no money made in your office. It's made by the hands of your team members. So you should spend as much time as possible engaged and participating in their processes. If you don't do it, you don't believe it! It is that **simple. Get in the fox hole with your team and fight with them during tough times!**

This also requires you to think about the how your company wants to be perceived in the work place and in the community. It's the way you dress-yes your appearance speaks volumes of how you lead and operate your company. If you are sloppy, out of shape or not well groomed, your teams, groups and team members will follow. It's "All eyes on me" although not the same as the classic Tupac Shakur song but it's true. From the moment you walk in the door in the morning until you leave in the evening, you are being look at in all facets. So a great leader should represent or model what he wants others to follow.

Creating this connection with your team will build trust and I believe that you should support them and understand them during the up and downs of the business.

Each day, you should do a mirror check before you leave for work.

1.    Appearance – Check yourself (Do I look the part today?)
2.    What are my key 3 things I want to reinforce today?
3.    Who will I recognize today for doing an outstanding job

## CONFIDENCE

If you are modeling what you want your company to be, your confidence will show. One of my heroes is Colin Powell. I have had the pleasure of meeting him and listening to his great leadership advice. The one thing that he mentions is that if your team trusts you and have confidence in you, they will follow you if for nothing else, out of curiosity. This means your team will truly believe that you will have their backs in times of trouble, and you will reward them during the good times with their fair share of the company's success. So how do you build confidence that your team will follow? Well, it starts by being transparent about your strengths and weaknesses and allowing the smartest guy in the room to make some decisions at will. The last thing you want as a leader is to be the smartest person in the room on all topics.

I have a Sean-ism that is very important when you are a leader and that is being "Bomb Proof." Bomb Proof relates to how a person acts when the situation is at a crisis level, and how that person acts when the waters are calm. Being Bomb Proof means that you will conduct your business with a level head no matter what the situation. Your team will model this consistency and follow your lead because they can trust that you are not making rash decisions that may jeopardize the company.

When dealing with crisis, use a calm damage-control voice and attitude. Your team will pick up on that feeling. The key objective is to keep everyone working and moving ahead.

## ARE WE HAVING FUN YET?

The top 3 reasons your high potential employees will leave your company are:

> *The Leader or Leadership Team*
> *Their Career Development*
> *Lack of Company Pride*

You may have noticed money did not make the top 3?

Why would the number one reason be their leader? You ask some really good questions. It's really simple; team members want to feel valued, respected and most importantly, they want to have autonomy in their jobs. You are going pay all that money to recruit, train and provide resources, why not lead them how you would want to be led?

If team members don't feel valued and just do as they are told to avoid rocking the boat, then the company does not grow. This kind of culture lacks innovation and stifles creativity as team members are too scared to come up with new ideas or challenge the status quo.

Team members want to feel like they are a part of something special, they want to be engaged, respected, and not micro managed. Why do companies spend thousands of dollars recruiting and training team members not let them do their jobs with trust and flexibility?

The key question is; are you having fun yet? It sounds simple, but you must create an environment in the 21$^{st}$ century that promotes activity, recognition, flexibility autonomy with each member.

## KEY POINTS:

1. Let them Fly

2. Feed forward and not feedback (If Feed forward is done properly all the coaching is done upfront, so there is no need to feedback!)

3. Schedule brain storming meetings once per week (2 hours of uninterrupted time that your team members can create on their own with no interruptions) --- Without your input and act on their ideas

4. What is recognized gets repeated

5. Someone may have a better idea than you do

# S - SERVANT LEADERSHIP

## moves more rocks than a bull dozer

Reading that quote from the legendary Maya Angelou above should be all you need to hear about being a servant leader. However, if you still need some support with this concept, I would start by saying that you'll have to want this style. If you need to learn it, it's going to test your soul.

First, start with trying to foster **humility**. Team members love it when you teach them something and show that you care about them doing it. Humility is something that needs to be practiced regularly. By acknowledging fallibility and the limits of one's own knowledge, the servant leader helps facilitate a learning environment and promotes team work to achieve goals.

Second, you must display **Authenticity.** It's a significant factor as it shows your team members you are acting with integrity, consistency, and that you have some morality about you. This can be done very simply by living your company's Mission and Vision and not creating your own that may differ slightly. It's done by sharing some personal stories of struggle and growth to show that you are also human.

## KEY POINTS:

1. Promote a culture of "Teaching and Not Telling" It is so easy to tell the team what to do. Anybody can do that

2. Be Real – Show some emotion

3. Support your team by doing and work together with them on some projects

4. Create your own personal action plan for leading selflessly

5. Practice listening with no action taken --- Just confirm you hear it and keep rolling. This is one of hardest things a leader can do---Listen attentively

6. Don't ruin the recognition by saying "Well done, but…." It shows no compassion and it shows you are all about your own agenda

7. Damn it- Help your team! Be an active participant

Lastly, understand what situational leadership is and practice it. You cannot lead with a one-size-fits-all mentality. Yeah, we know that a company should treat all members the same, but it's not the reality in most work places. Solid leaders will learn what moves each member of the team and support development, growth and opportunities based on that knowledge.

New School:  Ask, "What can I do to help you succeed?"

Old School:  Ask, "How can you help the company succeed?"

We all know the "Bottom Line" is the key to every company's profitability or all of our jobs are in jeopardy, but we must also think about the strengths and weaknesses of all members to maximize their performance which will in turn enhance the company's performance.

## KEY POINTS:

1.  Don't assume you know what motivates your team, find out person by person

2.  Ask them the top 5 priorities in their lives professionally and personally

3.  Act on them!

4.  Meet with your team members on a monthly basis to talk about them, not the company. You must separate the company's objectives from team members during these individual growth meetings.

## ▌ TOOLS:

Start and Stop Matrix:  This will give you the ability to ask your team specific value add or non-value add key things to work on. Do this with your direct reports quarterly. See appendix --- This is a quick and simple assessment tool that you can give your team for understanding if you are providing the support needed.

Simple Career Development Plan: Everyone in your organization should have one no matter what the job or title.  Smile and ask your team every day: "How can I make your job better?" The key is you must really mean it!

See Appendix for examples:

# M - MONEY MAKER!

## You must get results-
## It Is built on teamwork
## and new opportunities

The first half of this book helps to establish a base line of leadership that is required for sustainability.  It is setting the foundation or providing an environment of "Leadership with Care."  If these things are done right, and you have made enough deposits (demonstrated your credibility, reliability, and know how), you can start the process of getting the results you need to take your company to the next level.

Now we need to talk about why your company hired or promoted you into this role in the first place.

Someone saw the potential in you that would help take your company to the next level and most importantly, to gain market share for the stakeholders and meet the profit goals of the company. In other words, "Show me the Money." I promise you this, if you are not getting the results, smart companies will find someone who will. I have always made sure that results are paramount in the companies that I have worked, and one way is to ensure that there is a strong Mission and Vision no matter how big or small your company or department.

You must be able to answer the following questions:

1.  What are we doing as a company or team?

2.  Why are we doing it as a company or team?

3.  Where does your team fit into the overall company's strategy?

4.  If we did not exist would anybody miss us?

5.  What is your customer's number one expectation of the company?

This process will make or break you and prove that your leadership team made the right decision hiring you and/or promoting you to your current position. It will also prove whether the KISS My @#$ stuff works or not? I know the top 3 items (KIS) seems very simple but please keep in mind that clear directions and a concise plan must be set that all members of the organization can follow to get results.

***If there is one thing that I have learned during my time as a leader, it is that if you have too many priorities; you have zero priorities – Sean-ism.  It's important that your team know that you have a stable approach, a firm foundation, a priority of what to attack. 100 priorities equal 0 priorities.

Your team is looking for a solid balance of the stretch goals (a goal that is slightly beyond what you think you can achieve) and common goals that they have the capacity to achieve.

A great leader must focus on the few chosen objectives to make a significant impact. Great leaders have a passion for getting their teams to focus on the "Most Important" goals and reducing the clutter that distracts them from achieving those goals.

How?

**Do the 2's!!!** There are 2 important items in each category that should be identified and the focus should be directed there.

**What are the 2 outcomes for your day**----who will be the champion (Accountability) and how will you measure success?  Yes 2 people ! not 10, 20 …. No matter how many people you are responsible for leading.

**What are the 2 outcomes for your week**---- who will be the champion (Accountability) and how will you measure success?

**What are the 2 outcomes for your month**---- who will be the champion (Accountability) and how will you measure success?

**What are the 2(core strategic priorities) outcomes for your year**--- who will be the champion (Accountability) and how will you measure success?

You and your team should be able to visualize these achievable goals each day. The small wins will eventually equal your team's large wins and you will be on your way to achieving your company's vision.

Ok you have a mission and vision, now you can start the process of your attack planning. (Simply Lead)

Start with your major projects by Key Performance Indicator and create VISUALIZATION that your entire team can see "What and How?" you will attack.

Ideas --- See Appendix for a simple 1-year planning document

# Y - YOU!

## If you don't do it, you don't believe it! Sean-ism

When I started this journey with you, I made a very important request? If you don't wake up every morning with a *smile* on your face and a firm belief that your team will make a significant difference today due to your leadership, you should stop reading this book and perhaps change jobs. You may be cheating your company and your team.

**You** are the most important person to your success. If you are the type that blames the company for not giving you the training, mentorship, roadmap, career development or pay, then your team will think the same way.  Now is the time for **You** to take on the challenge of being a high powered leader.

You have heard the old saying, "Lead people like you would want to be led." But, not so fast my friend; you may be a T-Rex type of leader who believes that "It's my way or the highway" or you may be a push over leader who says I let my team fly until they fall.

The "**You**", I am talking about is the person who is consistent with his tongue. You are the example of how the company vision should be executed. You value all people regardless of race, gender, size or sexual orientation.  The more time spent on the floor walking, talking, learning and understanding the company business will be vital to your success.  It is difficult to gain a true understanding sitting behind a desk. You must be an active leader.  You will be recognized as a great leader if you are able to sincerely submit to the following:

> The 6 most important words: I admit I made a mistake.
>
> The 5 most important words: You did a great job.
>
> The 4 most important words: What do you think?
>
> The 3 most important words: Could you please?
>
> The 2 most important words: Thank you!
>
> The most important word: We.
>
> **The least important word: I."**
>
> **Unknown Author**

Great leaders know that it all starts with them. Your team will monitor everything that you say and do.  Good leaders are always on audition no matter how long you have been with the company.

## KEY POINTS:

1. My Talk ----- It will tell others what I value and believe

2. My Walk---- It will show others how committed I am to the company's goals and objectives

3. I got you---- Will I take a stand for what is right or will I waver under pressure?

4. Perform a Personal Inventory (PI) each week
   a. Did I exhibit the company's values this week?
   b. Was I an example for others to follow?
   c. Could others see success in me?
   d. Did I lead by example?
   e. Did I make myself available?

Your team wants to see a sermon rather than hear a sermon; they want to know that you have their backs when times get rough.

Lastly and the most important point of the **"You"** is **"You"** must have integrity. It's paramount in all great leaders. It's **"You"** no matter what the circumstance or situation you maintain. It's your value system. How many times have you heard of corruption in corporate America at the highest level of the organization? It's rampant because these so-called leaders lack integrity. If you want to separate yourself from the status quo, do the right thing every time.

"Integrity is doing the right thing when no one is watching" The reason most of the corrupt leaders get caught is because someone is always watching!

*Sean Marcellas*

# A -ATTITUDE

## (the engine)

*Attitude can shift the tide for all companies, leaders and team members. The example we should all remember is your attitude can make you kick ass, be an ass or be an **ASSet** to your company and team.*
*Sean-ism*

Here is the Attitude check for your team --- Would they say the following about you?

1.  He/she **Listens** and is **Approachable**
2.  He/she uses my Ideas
3.  He's/she's **Encouraging**
4.  He's/she's an **Example** of the Ideal Condition
5.  He/she **Breeds** positive team members
6.  He's/she's **Not** the smartest person in the room
7.  He/she **Goes** above and beyond

## IT BEGINS WITH THE BATTERY (ATTITUDE)

Without electrical current, you might as well remove your car's wheels and prop it up on concrete blocks on the lawn. Your car is an electrical machine, and the battery is what gives it life.

Most car batteries are the lead-acid variety, and their primary job is to leap into action as soon as you turn the key in the ignition. This causes a weak electrical current to flow from the battery to a solenoid or relay.

The starter motor begins a process that turns the flywheel and the crankshaft and subsequently, the pistons. The pistons draw a combustible fuel/air mixture, a spark plug provides ignition and presto — your car's engine starts, and your battery's biggest task is, for the moment, complete.

Ok, enough of the car - talk, attitude is just like a car battery, without a positive or forward thinking attitude, your team or company will not move. They will stay in the same place year after year.

It is very important that you are the attitude "Super Model" for your organization or team. I am telling you it's contagious if you do it correctly or incorrectly.

Lastly, find yourself **attitude scouts** on your team. This should be someone who has the pulse of the organization and will give you honest feedback on your attitude impact and can offer suggestions on change.

You already know those who exhibit positive attitude traits. Smile, thank you, congrats, I can, I support……..

*Leaving a legacy is all about leaving repeatable systems that are easy to implement and" Kaizen"*

*- continuous improve Sean Marcellas*

# S -SYSTEMS

## (Sustainable, growth, legacy...)

Born in Nashville, TN in 1952, Bill Belichick (New England Patriots Head Coach) has revolutionized the game of football with a NFL winning percentage of 70% of his games during the regular season, 4 Super Bowl championships spanning over 15 years. He became the first head coach to ever preside over a 16-0 regular season team. He has more playoff wins than any other coach in NFL history. So what is his secret for success? How is he able to perform at such a high level year after year with the average player in the NFL only lasting 3.3 years on avg.?Statista.com

It's his systems!!!!

His 5 Key components for his football team's success are the following:

*Study* --- *His preparation for games is unmatched*

*Strategy* --- *His ability to game plan and execute with agility is legendary*

*Strength*--- *He focuses on the team strengths and not their weaknesses (example his Hall of Fame quarterback runs the 40 in about 6 secs, and for those who don't know, that is very slow! Instead of focusing on this weakness, he focused on the strength of his quarterback's arm)*

*Sustain* ---- *From the first day of training camp to the preparation for the super bowl, his team's regiment and routines are followed to the letter, leading to victory.*

*Sacrifice* ---- *It's been said that during the football season, Bill will only get about 4 hours of sleep per night.*

These same 5 key components can also apply to your teams and company. To develop systems that can carry your team to the next level and be sustained!

**Study** --- Understanding your competition can be done with a thorough company SWOT – Strength, Weakness, Opportunities and Threats analysis. Having a complete understanding of your talent base strengths and weaknesses is also vital in studying your company's current position.

Example:

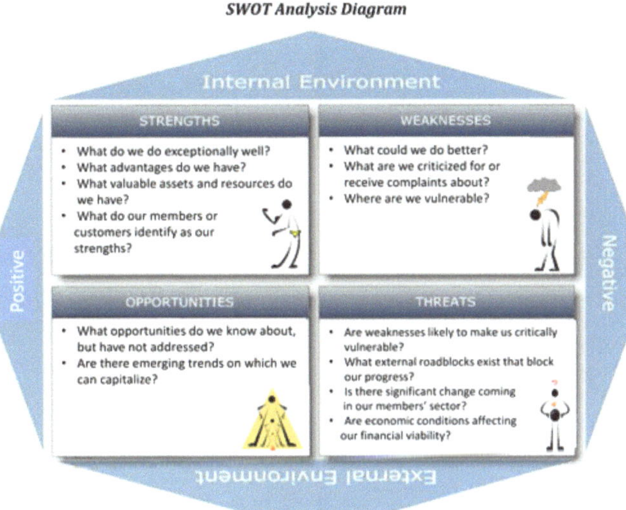


**Strategy** --- Development of short-term, intermediate, and long-term planning that supports your company's overall objectives and makes them easy to understand at all levels.

**Strength**--- Make sure to continue doing the great things and do not let them slide while trying to implement the new. (Maximize what you do well.) Build on the 85% of excellence by recognizing it and rewarding it. Your team's strengths will get you through and help you achieve the other 15%

**Sustain** ---- The focus is **"Being Brilliant at the Basics."** It will carry your company in the highs and lows. This means, following your company's operating procedures consistently, Leadership development consistently, and voice of the customer management systems consistently. Just to name a few. Remember Belichick.

**Sacrifice** ---- This is about going the extra mile to make your team members and customers feel valued through personal engagement, recognition and being there for them in times of need.

This may also require you to flex your shift to talk to off shift team members or attend meetings that you are not required to attend but, are doing so to support your team.

This also includes being a continuous learner, through books, training, and company sponsored events. (You know like reading my book again and telling your friends about it!)

# S-SUCCESSION

## You need be an Elevator Operator!

**"If you want 1 year of prosperity, grow grain. If you want 10 years of prosperity, grow trees. If you want 100 years of prosperity, grow people"**

**unknown Author**

So why is this so important?

Without commitment to this proactive process, many companies are likely to remain reactive. As a result, leaders will find themselves conducting executive searches and interviewing outsiders.

**The "Oh Crap" will happen.** No matter how good you and your staff are at revenue projections or economic predictions, no one can truly plan for a disaster. Whether it's an unforeseen illness, a natural disaster, or a CEO's decision to suddenly retire, the reasons for having a succession plan in place before it is needed are endless. So while you can't plan for disaster, you can put into place a series of contingencies that will help your company stay afloat if, in fact, a catastrophe occurs.

- **Succession planning should be proactive not reactive.** Just as business practices have evolved over the years, succession planning has also grown and changed. It's no longer a plan that can only be accessed when leadership is going to change; a succession plan can be used before its "real" intent if necessary. It can be used to build strong leadership, help a business survive the daily changes in the marketplace, and force executives to review and examine the company's current goals.

- **Succession planning shows your leadership that they are valued.** If you're running a family business, the process of succession planning will give family members an opportunity to express their needs and concerns. Giving them a voice will also help create a sense of responsibility throughout the organization, which is critical for successful succession planning. Resist the temptation to solely carry the entire weight of creating and sustaining a plan.

- **Succession planning is for long-term thinkers.** Some companies mistakenly focus solely on replacing high-level executives. A good succession plan can go further, however, forcing you to examine all levels of employees. The people who do the day-to-day work are the ones keeping the business going. Neglecting to add them to the succession planning mix could have dire consequences. As you develop your plan, incorporate all layers of management and their direct reports.

- **Get over yourself and let someone else have it!** A major component of a succession plan is exciting and can bring a company unforeseen rewards. Still, change can be a source of tremendous stress, especially when people's livelihoods are at stake. As you put your succession plan together, consider its positive effects on the business. Planning for the future is exciting, and, if done correctly, can inspire your workers to stay involved and maintain company loyalty. It's true that a plan is often put into place to avert catastrophe, but it's also a company's way of embracing the future—a business strategy that is essential for survival.

*"If you want **1** year of prosperity, grow grain. If you want **10** years of prosperity, grow trees. If you want **100** years of prosperity, grow people"*

*Unknown Author*

Well I know that is a lot of information in a short amount of time. So your questions maybe where do I start? Or how do I know I can get these things done?

My advice to you would be to use all 9 key components step by step. For example you can try to implement one key point per month from each of the 9 key components. It really starts with your ability to *Kindle* an organization and ends with you building a team and legacy.

These are very simple and practical examples that are proven to work if you take the time do them.

The appendix shows you some examples that could be used to help support you in leadership journey. Use them and follow the book. Remember that continous improvement will help you propel your company, make these templates your own.

Thanks for giving me an hour or so of your time. Now get back to work, LEADER!

Sean Marcellas

> "Lead unto others as you would have them lead
> unto you"
>
> Sean Marcellas

# SIMPLE TEMPLATES

(See Appendix for example if you need it--- first 90 days)

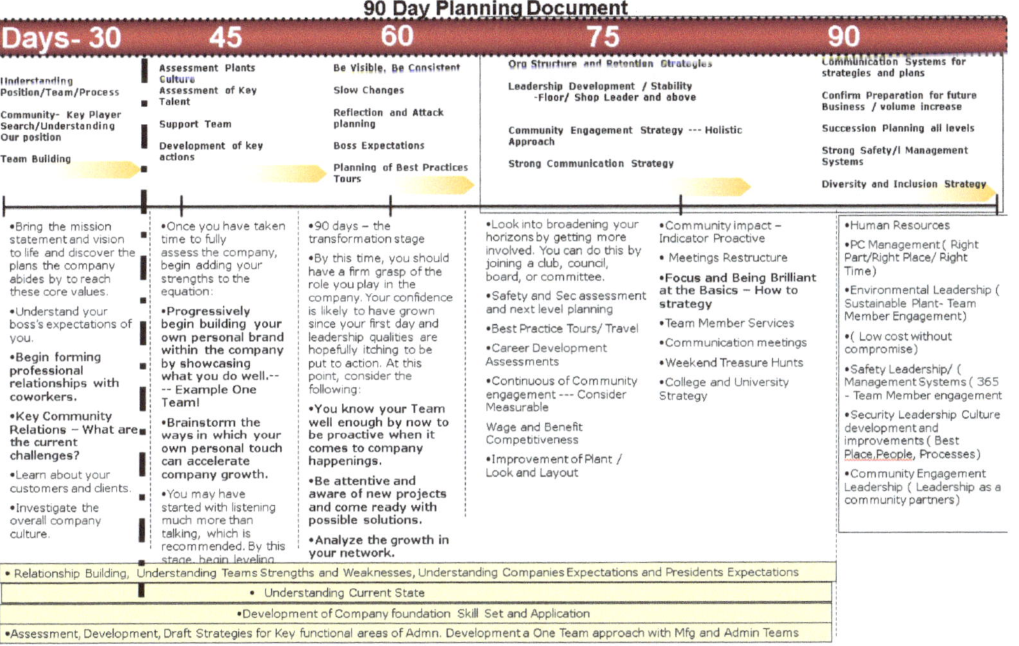

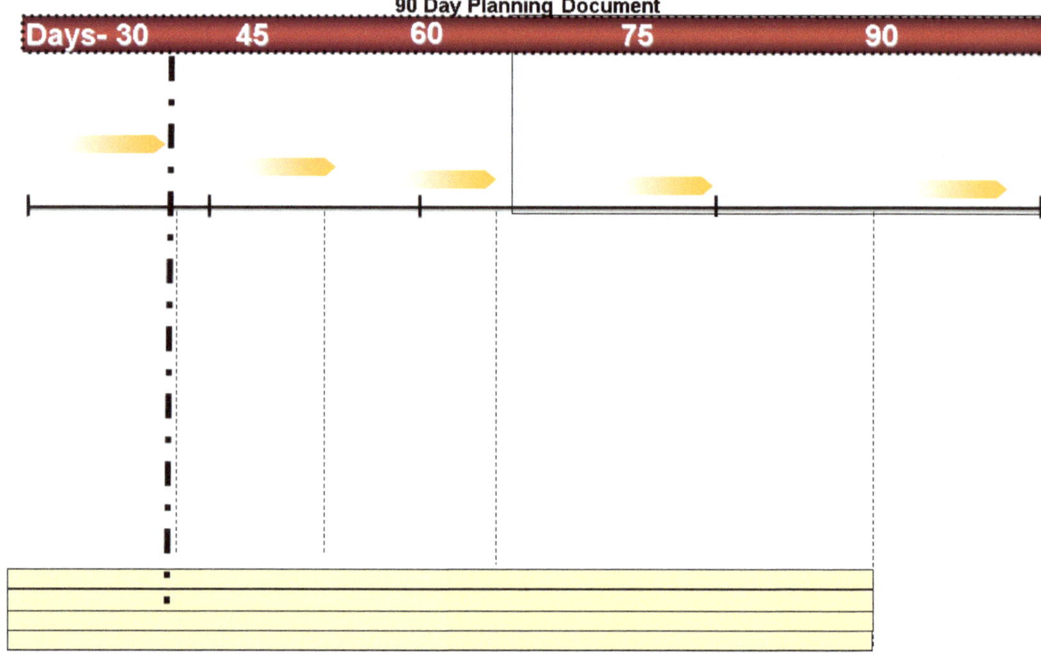

90 Day Planning Document
Days- 30
45
60
75
90

# Vision Example

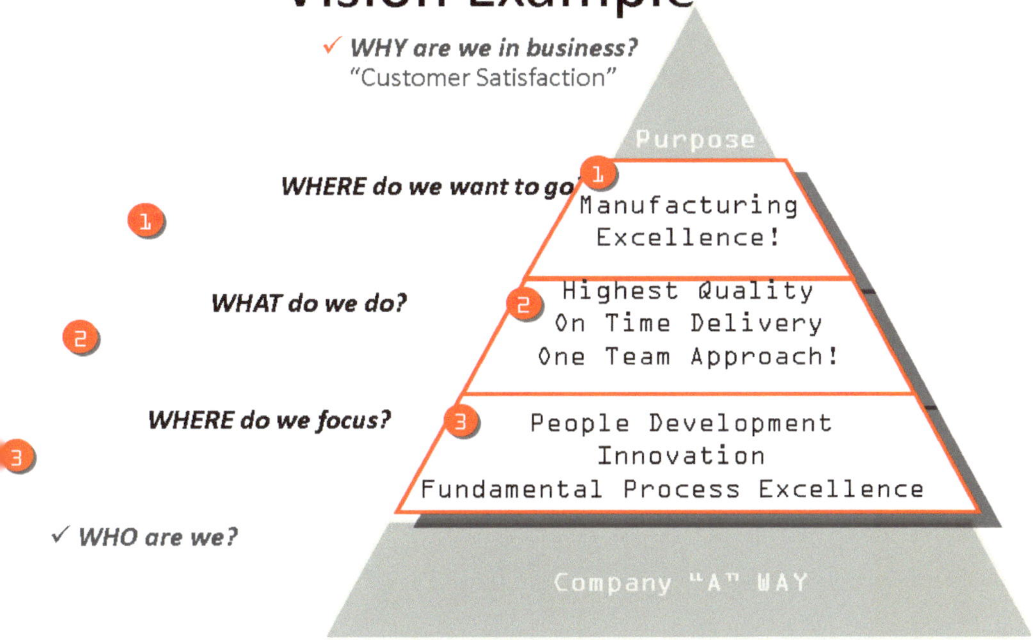

✓ *WHY are we in business?*
"Customer Satisfaction"

*WHERE do we want to go?*

**1**

*WHAT do we do?*

**2**

*WHERE do we focus?*

**3**

✓ *WHO are we?*

# Vision Example

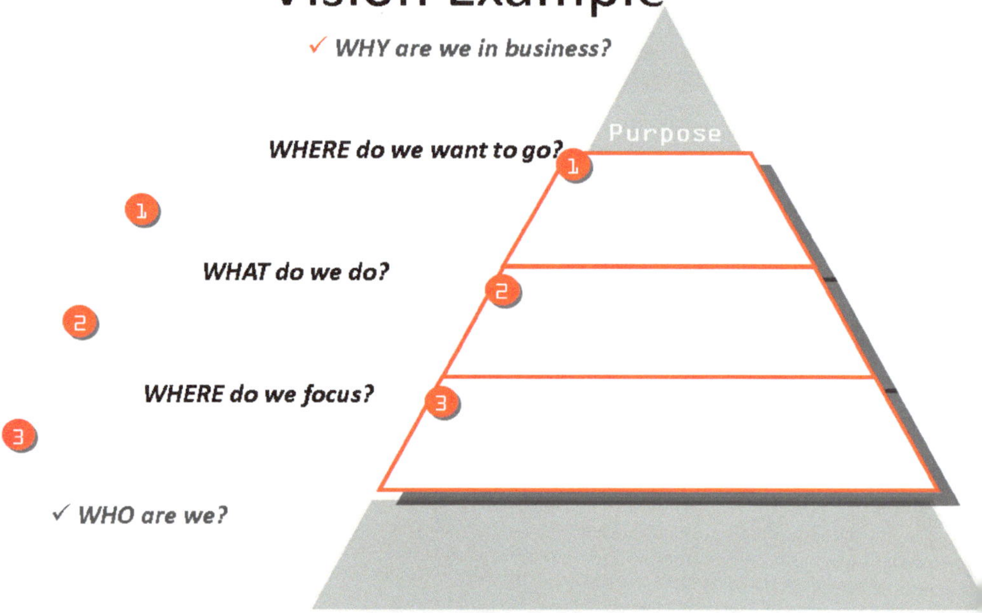

DO THE 2's !!

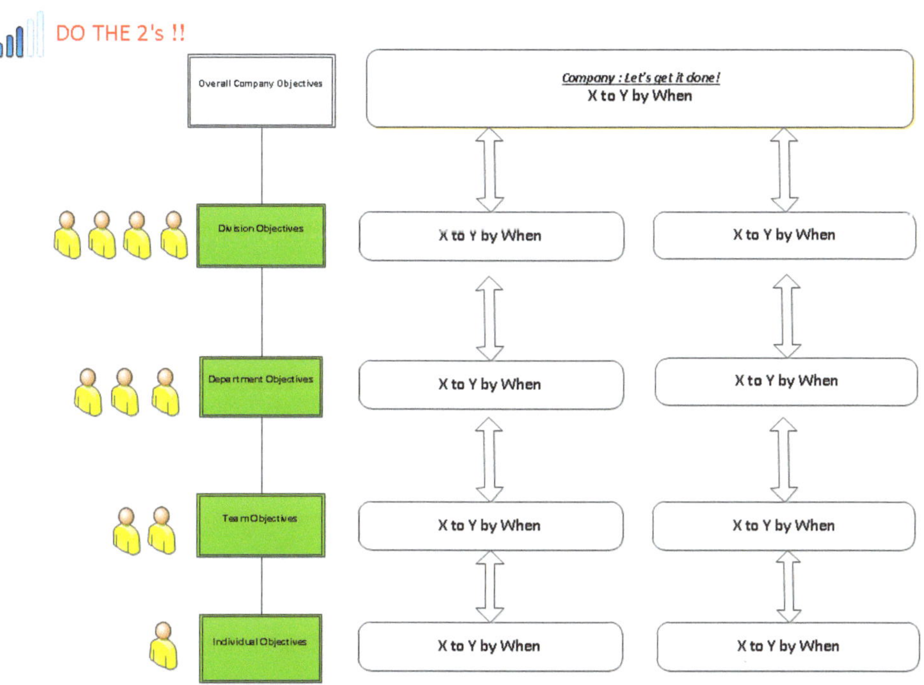
Overall Company Objectives
Division Objectives
Department Objectives
Team Objectives
Individual Objectives
Company : Let's get it done!
X to Y by When
X to Y by When
X to Y by When
X to Y by When
X to Y by When
X to Y by When
X to Y by When
X to Y by When
X to Y by When

# <u>Your Career Plan</u>

<u>Who You Are?'</u>

<u>Education</u>

<u>Employment etc.</u>

Personal / Hobbies

Values

Limitations/ Travel / Times

My Goals:

| <u>Short Term</u> | <u>Mid Term</u> | <u>Long Term  >5yrs</u> |
| --- | --- | --- |
| | | |
| | | |

<u>Current Skill Set and Strengths</u>

<u>Development----Techincal and Non Techincal</u>

<u>Action Plan/ How can your supervisor support?</u>

# DEVELOPMENT OF A 1-YEAR PLAN

Example of overall Company Goal
BASIC BUSINESS PLANNING
Core 4
Strategies
Activities
Measurable
Keep it Simple!!!!

Stop-Start- Continue  FEEDBACK

TM NAME: _____________________          TM Position: __________          DATE: __________________

      COST CENTER: __________     TM ID#                              SHIFT: __________________

STARTS
- 
- 
- 

STOPS
- 
- 
- 

CONTINUES
- 
- 
- 

SUPERVISOR NAME: _______________________________     Position: __________     DATE: _______________

      COST CENTER: __________     TM ID# __________                    SHIFT: _______________

STARTS
- 
- 
- 
- 
- 

STOPS
- 
- 
- 
- 
- 

CONTINUES
- 
- 
- 
- 
- 

ISSUES/CONCERNS:

_______________________________________________________________________________
_______________________________________________________________________________
_______________________________________________________________________________
_______________________________________________________________________________
_______________________________________________________________________________
_______________________________________________________________________________
_______________________________________________________________________________